singing into darkness

tanka and ryuka triptychs by Joy McCall and Liam Wilkinson

Copyright © 2017 Joy McCall and Liam Wilkinson

All rights reserved. No part of this book may be reproduced or transmitted in any form or by any means, electronic or mechanical, without permission from the authors.

ISBN-13: 978-1544190488

ISBN-10: 1544190484

published by
wildflower poetry press
www. wildflowerpoetrypress.wordpress.com
wildflowerpoetrypress@gmail.com

editor: Caroline Skanne

cover art: Marianne Paul (http://www.literarykayak.com/)

cover design: Caroline Skanne

a few words from the editor

Joy McCall and Liam Wilkinson — both outstanding poets and important voices in contemporary tanka and closely related short forms — have decided to share their correspondence of responsive sequences with the world. As a publisher this is an exciting event, as a reader even more so.

Infused with lyricism and deep meanings, these triptychs (sets of three poems), manage to somehow transcend the boundaries of here and now. This is a journey with no clear beginning or end; but rather a continuous thread of thoughts, memories and events leading us through the darkness, poem by poem, or if you prefer, song by song.

The pleasure of having played a part in the materialization of this book, however small, has been nothing short of immense. Thank you Joy, Liam and those who offering a helping hand on the way. I would also like to extend my thanks to Marianne Paul, who created the cover art for this book, skillfully incorporating the mood, colours and themes of *singing into darkness*, with both sensitivity and flair.

— Caroline Skanne

a shimmering thread...

Her name had been a familiar one for some time when I first wrote to Joy McCall back in 2015. I'd read her tanka in various publications, mostly thanks to M. Kei who had included her work in his excellent Atlas Poetica. Having recently got my hands on a copy of Hedgerows – Joy's 2014 collection of pentaptychs – I was moved to do something I very rarely do. This mostly quiet and hermit-like scribbler of small poems sent an email to M. Kei for the attention of Joy, simply to let her know that she was, without any shadow of a doubt, my favourite poet; that her root-entangled, earth-scented and myth-kissed pentaptychs comprised the finest and most affecting poetry I'd had the pleasure of reading.

To my delight, Joy wrote back and, to my surprise, did so with effervescent kindness and astonishing modesty. Her reply revealed genuine amazement that anyone would find her poetry so enchanting. Indeed, to this day, Joy insists that I am the better poet; an opinion I simply can never accept but a kindness I feel so privileged to receive.

A long correspondence began. And whilst our regular emails touch frequently upon the changing of the seasons, music, books, health, our mutual friends, art, flowers, the terror of raging wars, sadnesses of local tragedies, the madness of politicians, the beauty of ancient Asian poetry, the moon, our common love for good Scotch, mythology, standing stones and our dear English landscape, there exists in our emails a shimmering thread of responsive poetry. I might send a ryuka to Joy after seeing the crescent moon in the window beside my writing desk and, without any persuasion on my part, Joy fills the rest of the moon with a ryuka drenched in earthlight. Similarly, Joy might drop a tanka into my inbox which finds her tracing the rain-soaked brick weave in her yard and I'll be inspired to place some crisp autumn leaves along the path. Some of our most captivating conversations have happened in lines of poetry.

Somewhere along the way, and probably inspired by our mutual love of numbers and counting, Joy and I discovered a way of tying our poetry together in sets of three. It was Joy who suggested we call them "triptychs", reminding me of those three-panel narrative paintings that grace the altars of so many churches. As is Joy's wish, I write the first poem, Joy replies with the central second verse and I close it with a third. It's only then, when these three tanka or ryuka come together, that we start to see the magic. Whether intentional or not, the three small panels in our triptychs tell many fascinating stories, and so we continue to paint.

— Liam Wilkinson, North Yorkshire, Spring 2017

part 1
10 tanka triptychs

earthlight

what a delight it is
when, after so long,
I turn to Tachibana
and find
lines of my own

reading
Taigu Ryokan
late at night
here, too, the thief left behind
the thin crescent moon

amongst these gifts
from the muse
soft earthlight
let us fill the moon
with our songs

the kappa's bowl

from afar, she sees
the pocks of my mind
filling with rain
I go to my door and find
a cartload of scrolls

one falls from the cart
I untie the strings
and unroll
water spilling
from the kappa's bowl

on the mountain
a lake full of sky
sitting still
her gifts bring me here, daily
to empty, to fill

acorns

another symbol
of our friendship
ringing with light
this winding path
is strewn with acorns

*stepping high
over oak saplings
half-drunk
on acorn coffee
and red wine*

I ask if you believe
in ghosts
you point into the woods
and tell me
to listen

being

sleepless and weary
I ignite
a stick of incense
a figure in the smoke
sits down on my bed

stirring from sleep
in the wee small hours
faint starlight
an odd little being
perched on my bedrail

dark of dawn
soft lamplight paints
two faces
in the window
both of them mine

old paperbacks

the melancholic lean
of all these
old paperbacks
yellowing with years
of fingerless neglect

taking down
the one most tattered
it falls open
at a torn page:
he named the boat Polaris...

ink runs down
my heart
I am bound for home
with only a star
to steer me

to the summit

in the coffee shop
beside my cup
that small white pill
and beyond it
the steep incline of a day

I dare not
look to the summit
I am dizzy
broken bits of song
tumble about my head

and then
a familiar melody
a vibration
in my breast pocket
your call a kind of caffeine

these hearts

fleeting anger
burns my tongue
each feeble sorry
staggers out
sore and singed

we tear
the vows apart
yet again
we promise peace
while throwing spears

and when these
hearts lie
bruised and bleeding
you set the table
while I pour the wine

on the sand

rolled from hand to hand
a cold, grey stone
nothing special
just a silent reminder
of the tide crashing around me

once I was a small girl
caught by the currents
pulled under
tossed, grazed, on the sand...
it feels like that, again

with each sweep
of the lighthouse beam
I comb the shore
longing to hold you
safe and sound

sirens

hanging from a string
around her neck
a white turritella
heavy with the sound
of secrets

*stepping back
from the cliff edge
I turn a deaf ear
to the sweet song
of the sirens*

a sea fret
unravels at my feet
like a memory
a white wave
returns her to me

winter wind

another January
another year
should I learn
a new language
or an old silence?

reading poems
aloud in the dark
is that my own voice
or some ancient other
whispering in my head?

serpentine song
of the whistling
winter wind
I try to trap each melody
in the mouth of my book

part 2
10 ryuka triptychs

summer rain

from the shelter of the old oak
I let all my senses wander
out into the soft summer rain
far from these weary bones

in the tree hollow my child sleeps
while I sit alone on the hill
and the moving shadows grow long
and the small stream runs high

a gentle rumble of thunder
and a brief, distant lightning flash
my belly swells with contentment
and I, too, fall asleep

roaming

noon light falls soft on the cobbles
of these old city snickelways
for a moment I'm all alone
just the ghost of myself

roaming the byways and footpaths
through the flatlands and poppy fields
crows cawing in the hazel grove...
my Norfolk, roots and roof

still, the voice of the sea is strong
it laps at the kerbs and oak trees
it floods the forests and churches
constantly calling us

points of light

another day starts its engine
I watch it through a small window
whilst writing a brief epitaph
for last night's fading moon

I'm gazing at the indigo sky
as the stars begin to appear
one by one, until the heavens
are strewn with points of light

a blue glow at the horizon
if only I believed the tales
of another life after death
how young I would feel now

my final breath

world, let me breathe my final breath
at the edge of a raging sea
just another cold grey pebble
beneath the wide white sky

let the wild west wind take me in
when my heartbeat slows and is still
as I gather height I will drop
poems on the green fields

and let my lines be discovered
by the curious magpie beak
that searches the rough for stanzas
to feed its sombre blues

loose threads

I wish to mend your broken bones
and seal the cracks that cross your mind
but all I have is paper, ink
and little piles of lines

so weave those lines together, friend
the way you know so well to do
let them sing the song of marrow
of joint, hinge and sinew

the pen and I know all too well
these songs cannot be sung alone
I offer you these four loose threads
and we two shall be sewn

The Duchess

silhouettes of castle ruins
take bites from a low yellow moon
while down on the night-blackened beach
she strokes her salty tune

her body lay among the dunes
headless, half-buried in the sand
a sad end to a hooker's life...
killed by a lover's hand

but still her melody rises
enchanting each tree in the wood
and the Broads sing of the Duchess
the Yare darkens with blood

white water

now I have been swept out to sleep
the whales of my subconscious swim
in wide, wet circles around me
each with names I gave them

the mountain minnows inside me
swim the rapids, flashing silver
upstream, downstream – joy and sorrow
chasing the pale moonlight

slowly now, I lower my ears
beneath the rushing white water
and hear the years left inside me
the life in these bones yet

night after night

suddenly awake in black dawn
my face wet through with silent tears
what dream dragged me into sadness
and left me there to dry?

*night after night the same girl comes
and takes my crooked hand and sings
'come and dance with me, old woman'
oh flee, wild haunting girl!*

first light falling into my tears
makes jewels of their tiny globes
come, morning magpies, see them shine
steal them away from me

the shadows

a demon dances through the streets
of this rain-dark ancient city
his jet black fiddle coughing smoke
his song a howling wind

the black dog runs from house to house
panting, scratching at every door
woe betide he who goes outside
he'll be dead before dawn

around the fire we tell our tales
in our pockets sprigs of willow
they keep us safe from the shadows
that share these crackling flames

snowlight

snowlight flickering through the frost
that fogs my single small window
sprinkling soft grey flakes of shadow
into my cooling cup

on the cream wall, moving grey shapes –
the sun setting behind the oaks
my brandy espresso grows cold
I'm lost in the leaf dance

I light the tiny white tea-light
in the sandalwood Buddha's hands
and let myself be a small flame
fading silently out

part 3
10 tanka triptychs

wind off the water

a sprite
swapping styles
from coat to coat
the wind off the water
of the dirty old Thames

my small river
flooding over its banks
stealing dinghies
grass and duck eggs
a thief in the night

a pale half moon
rippling, leaf-like
in a puddle
I take a deep breath
and ink my quill

spring

there's a minimalist
within me somewhere
I just need to move
everything out of the way
to find him

there's
a woman of excess
inside me
hiding in the stark
tidiness of the room

another spring
in the rattlebag world
we clean
our little corners
of chaos

Cairnholy

silver sea light
spumes
at the stones of Cairnholy
the ghost of Galdus
shrouds my shoulders

the spectral hand
touches mine, bones
marking my skin
I lift the wine cup
'sláinte an Righ'

in my beard
white moonlight
tufts of thistledown
and a mouth, dark
with ritual incantations

('sláinte an Righ' Scots gaelic: health to the king)

the madhouse

where the madhouse
once stood
a line of frazzled oaks
try to shake the memories
from their heads

hunter's moon rising
over the dark woods
a stifled scream
a long shadow fading
into the night

lumbering
among broken bricks
the milk-white man
who doesn't know
he's a ghost

damp clippings

as if I knew
what I were doing
I tend to my worries
with a rusted rake
and a pair of bent secateurs

a small pile
of damp clippings
new shoots growing
out of the sides
of dead dreams

through the mist
of a weary mind
your gentle words:
no blade can cut me
out of your care

mountain cornflower

in my honour
she plants
mountain cornflower
this fulfilled wish
to be a shade of purple

frail roots
finding good soil
grow deep
the knapweed begins
her journey to the light

a glass of Merlot
in the garden
names of old friends
whispering
through the brick-weave

passages

the me I wish
one day to be
spilled
on pages
stiff with time

the side gate
where I carved
joy + tufu
is gone – a brick wall
shuts me out

the jade night sky
bursts silently
into lines
I dig
a passage to my past

specks of dreams

under a rough
draft of day
I stand at the sink
splashing, splashing
specks of dreams

scattered
splinters of bone
under my feet
the nightmare replays
the needle stuck

into the ink well
a nib, a finger,
a whole self
broken into
five lines of memory

once upon a time

waking from a dream
of paper-white
silence
all these little screens
ink-black

a blank page
of the old notebook
in fading pencil
just four words –
once upon a time...

there was a beach
dunes rising
in my mind
where I could leave
lines in the sand

burrow

what a delight it is
when, with a rasp,
I tell the world
I cannot leave
the hut of my mind

I burrow
deep underground
when pain strikes
the dark mole turns,
blind, deaf, unafraid

when you see me
emerging
in a soft velvet hide
let me come
slow to my senses

acknowledgements

Some of these poems have appeared in *Atlas Poetica, Skylark, the Bamboo Hut, Ribbons* and *Blithe Spirit*. We thank the editors for their acceptances.

the poets

Liam Wilkinson is the author of *Seeing Double: Tanka Pairs* (Skylark, 2016). He has been writing and publishing haiku and tanka for almost two decades and has recently found a new home in the four line ryuka. He has served as editor of *3Lights, Prune Juice, Modern Haiga* and *Englyn*. Liam lives in North Yorkshire, England.

Joy McCall is a paraplegic nurse who lives in Norwich, England. She has been writing tanka for more than 60 years, ever since she discovered the works of Ryokan in her school library. Lately she also writes ryuka, having been inspired by her friend Liam. She is the author of many books of poetry, probably too many.

Made in the USA
Lexington, KY
27 June 2017